Unicorn Coloring Book For Adults

....

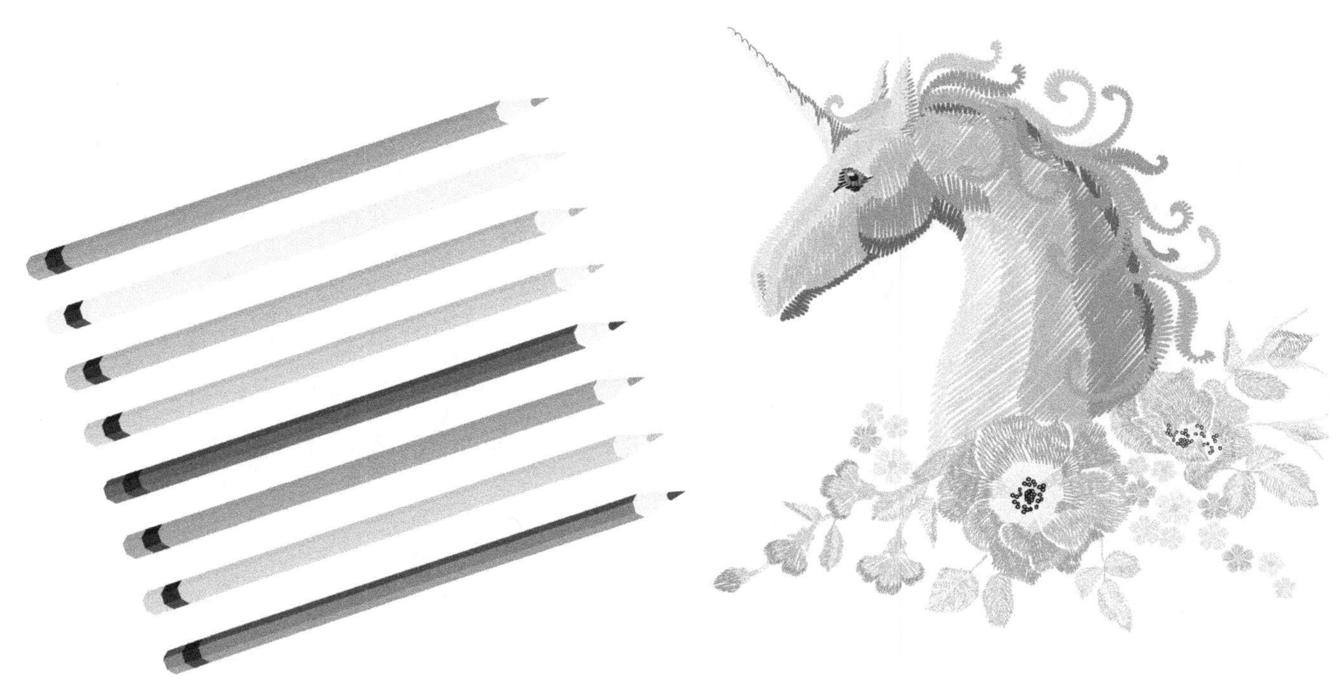

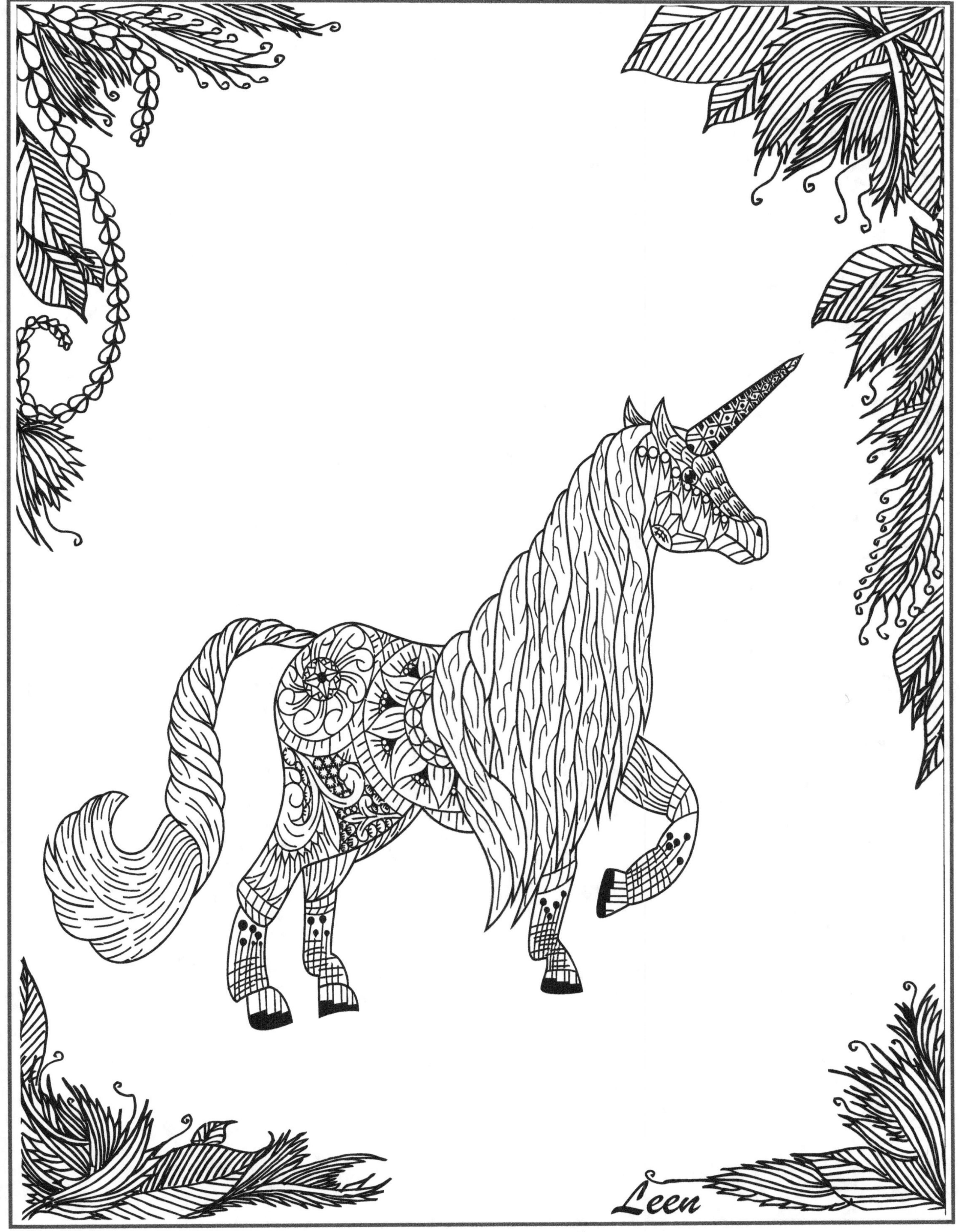
Leen

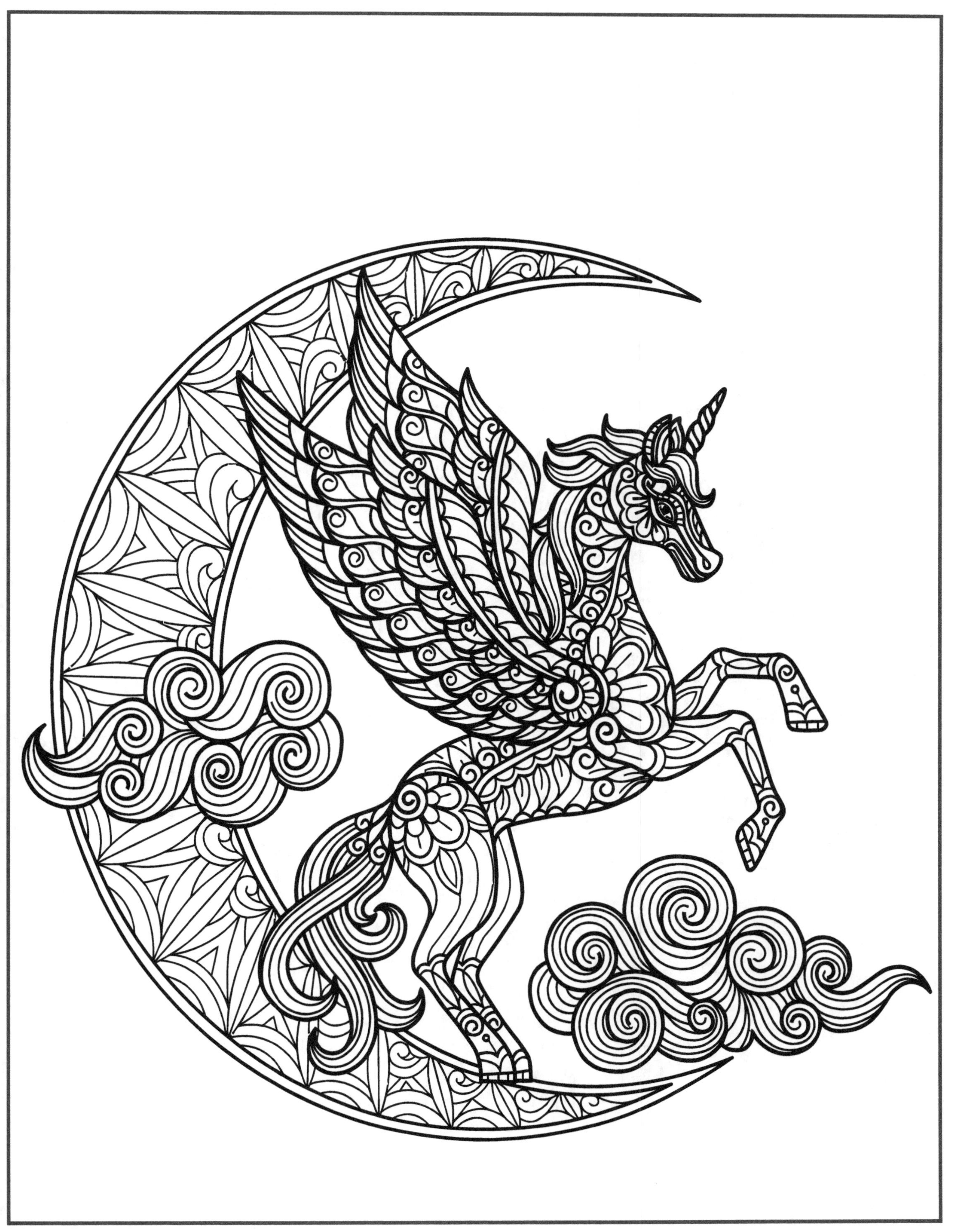

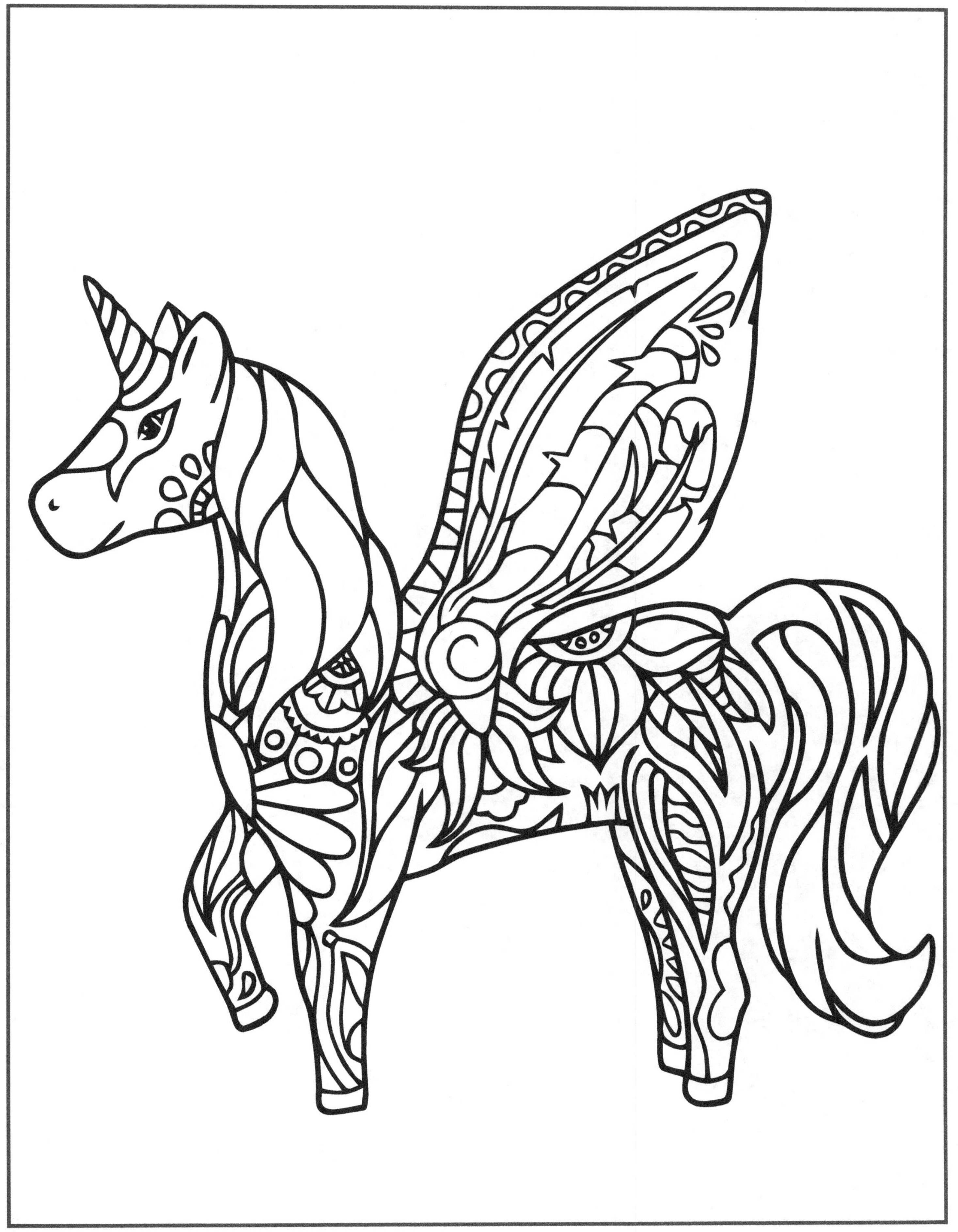

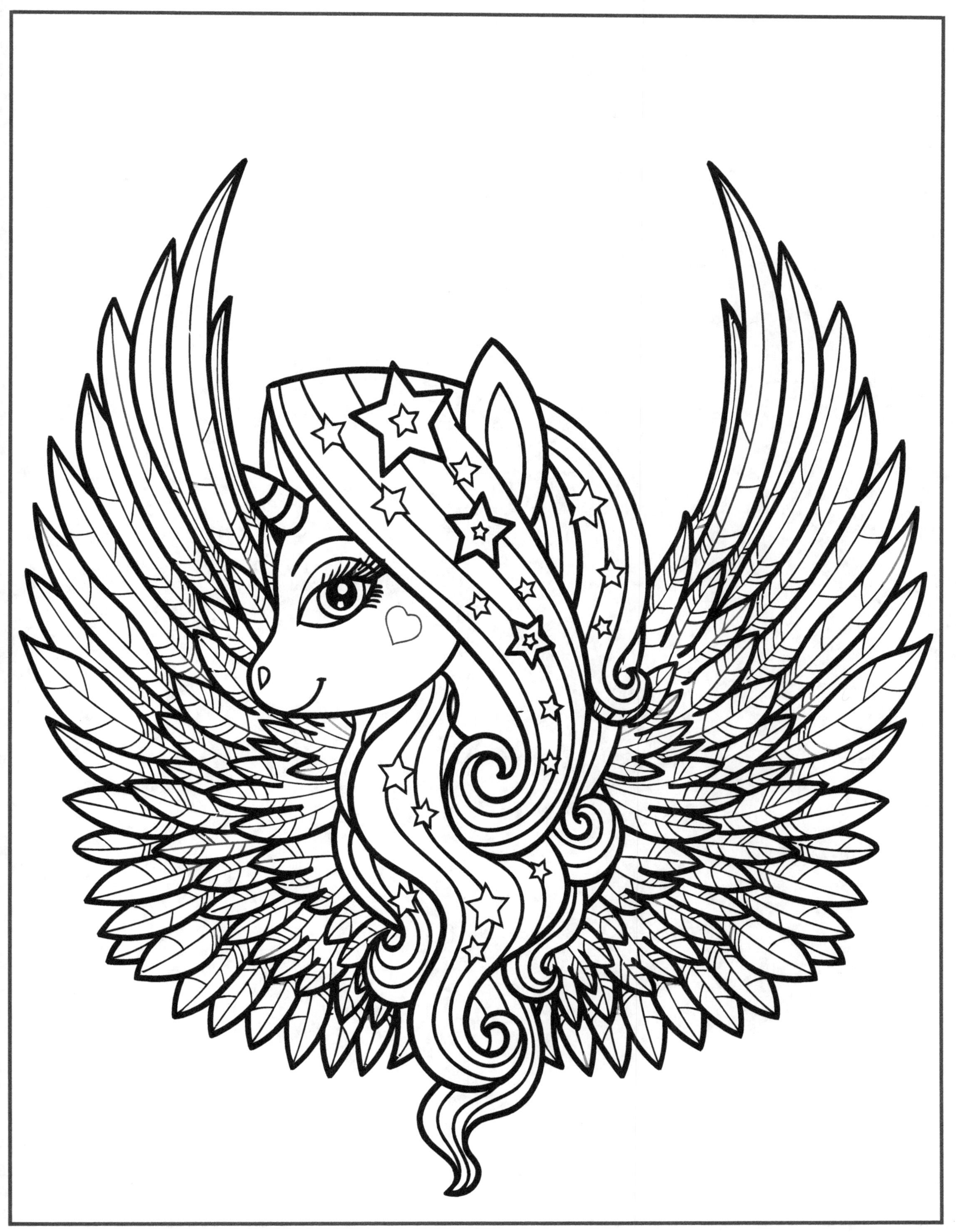

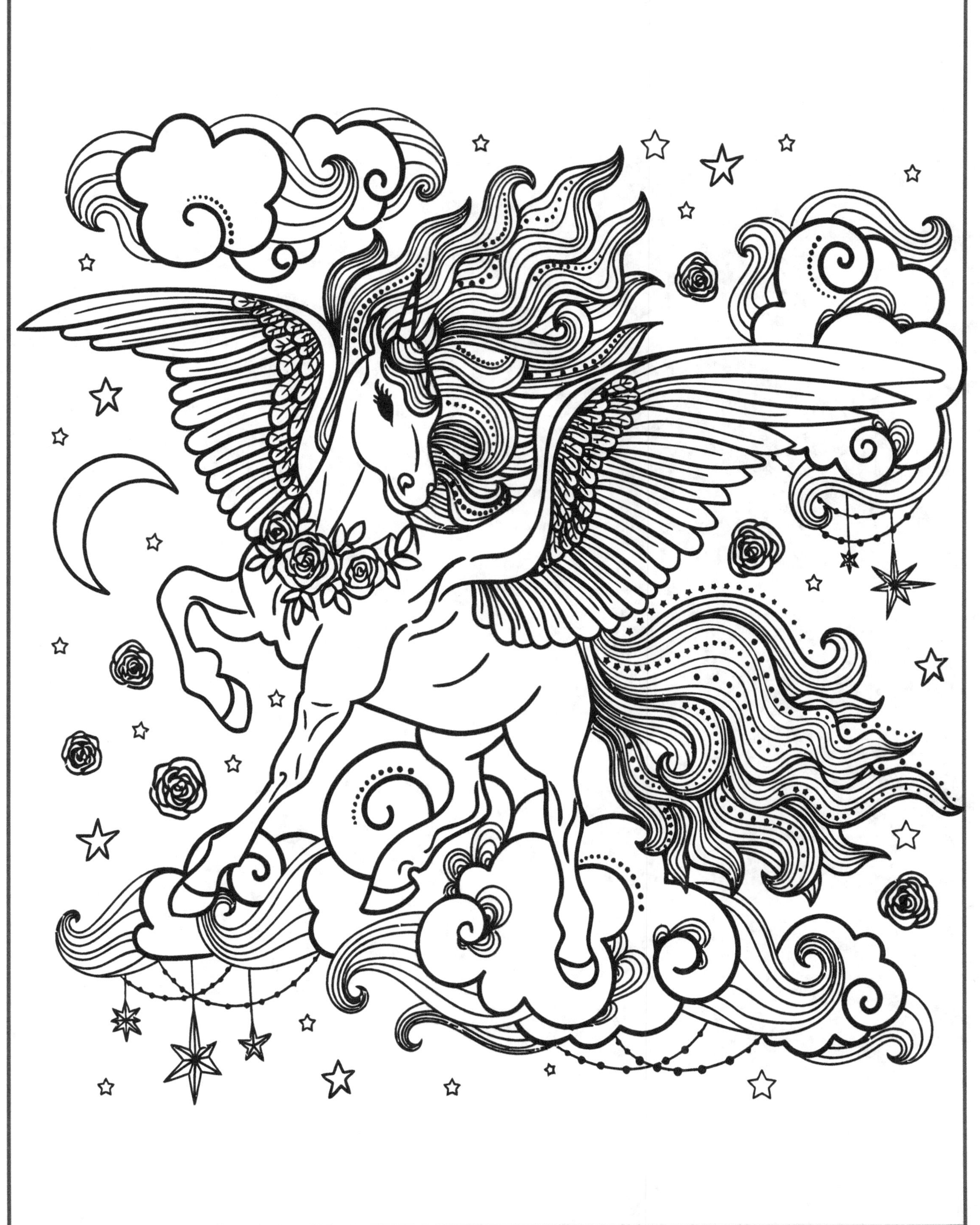

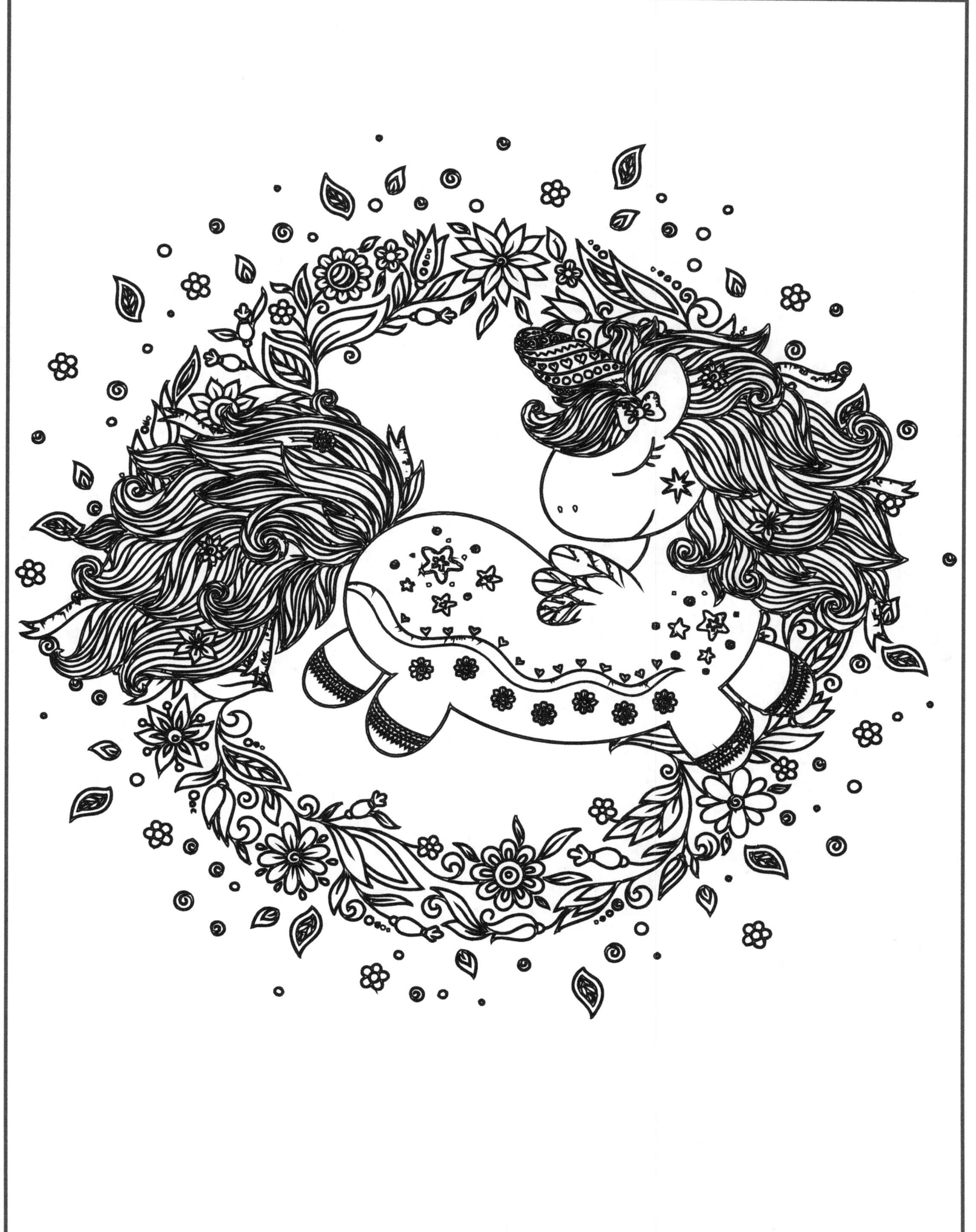

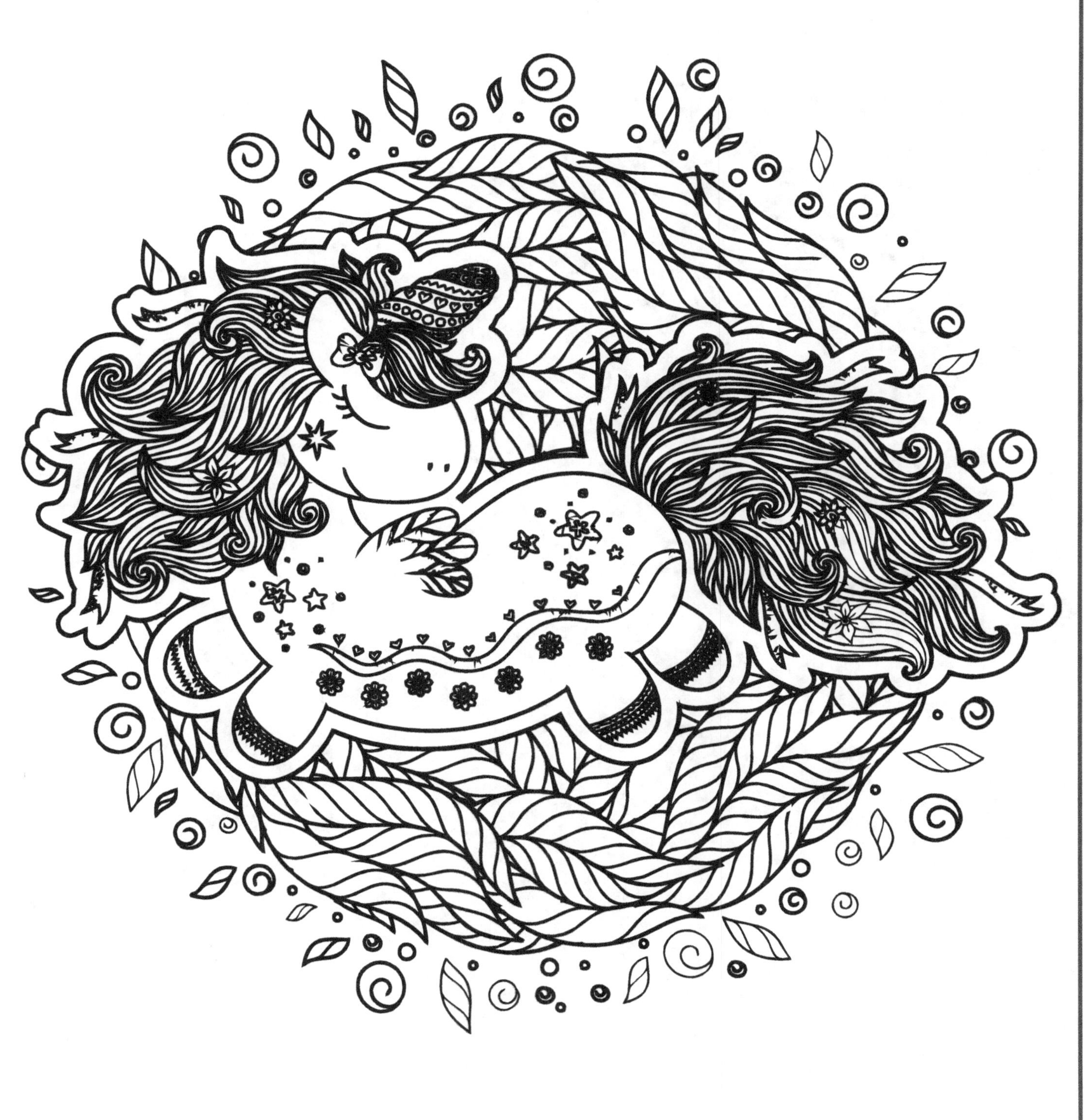

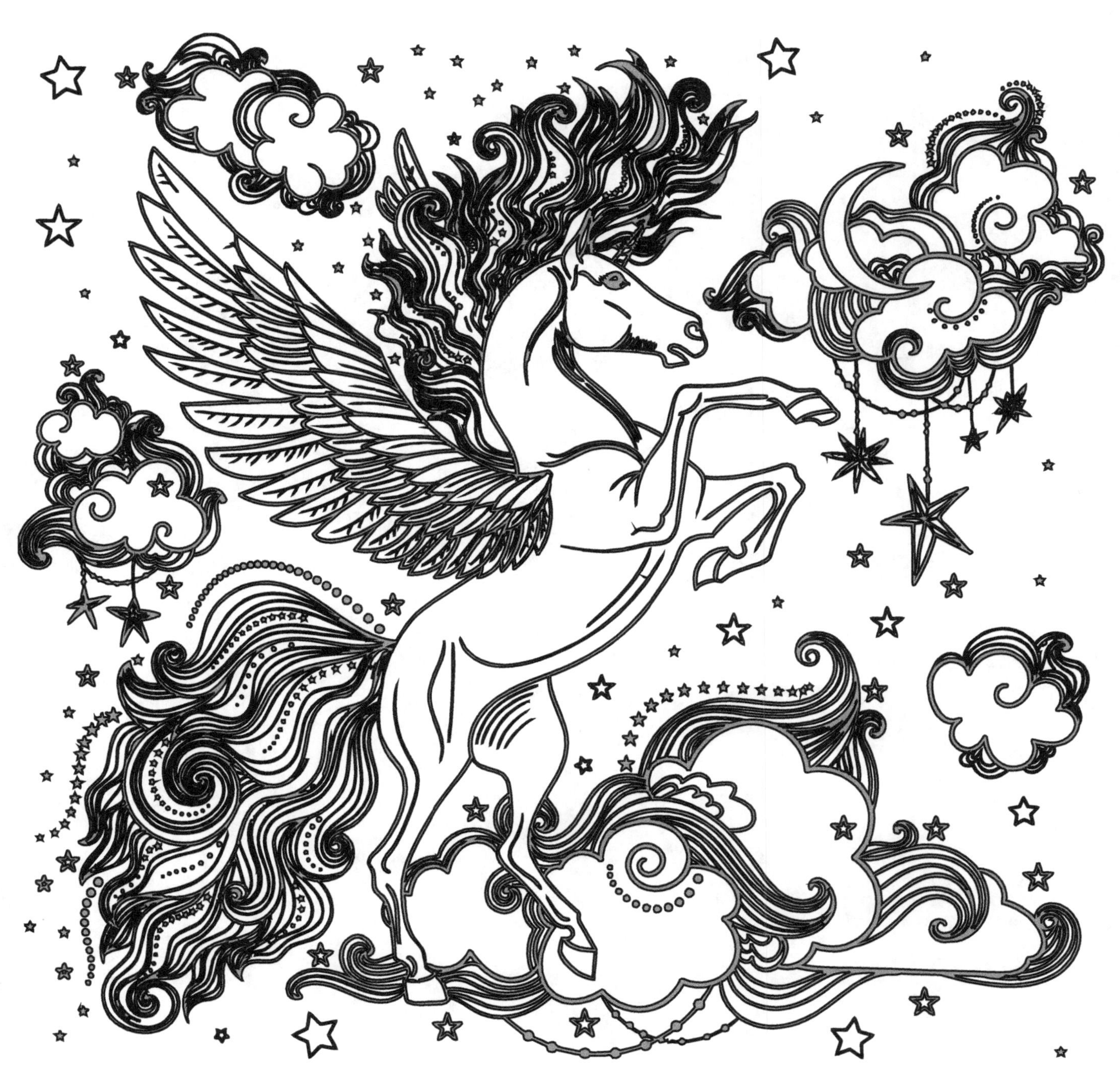

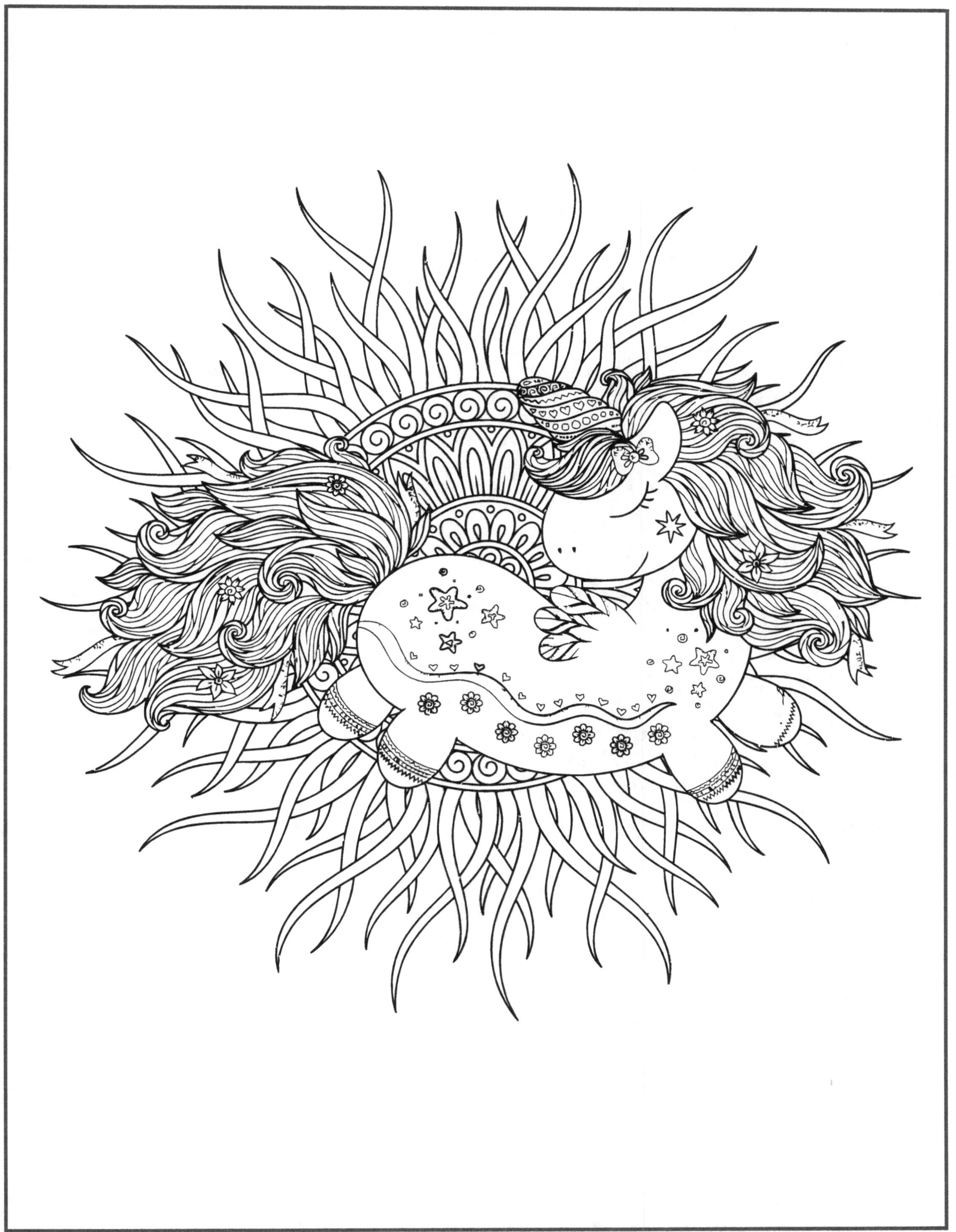

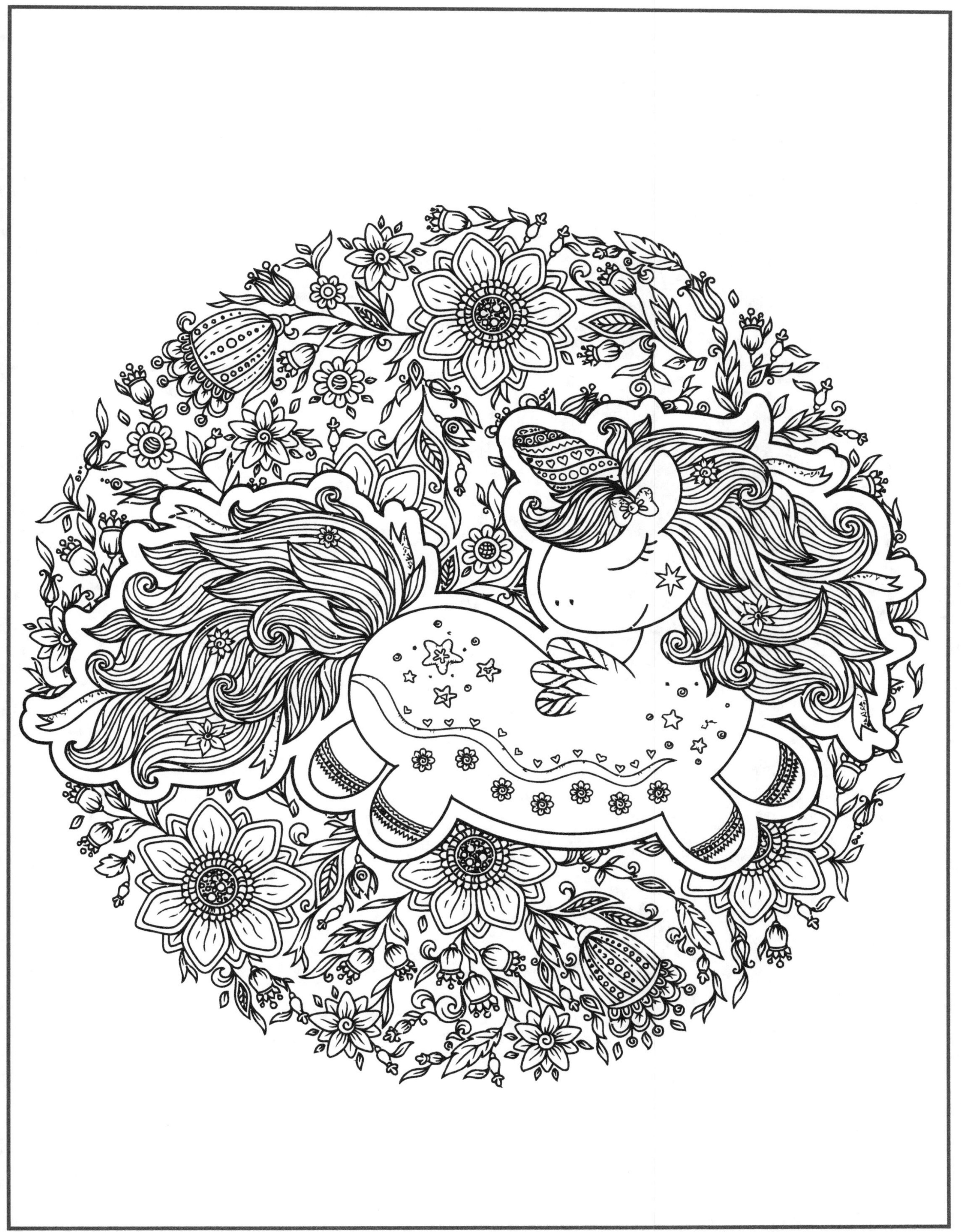

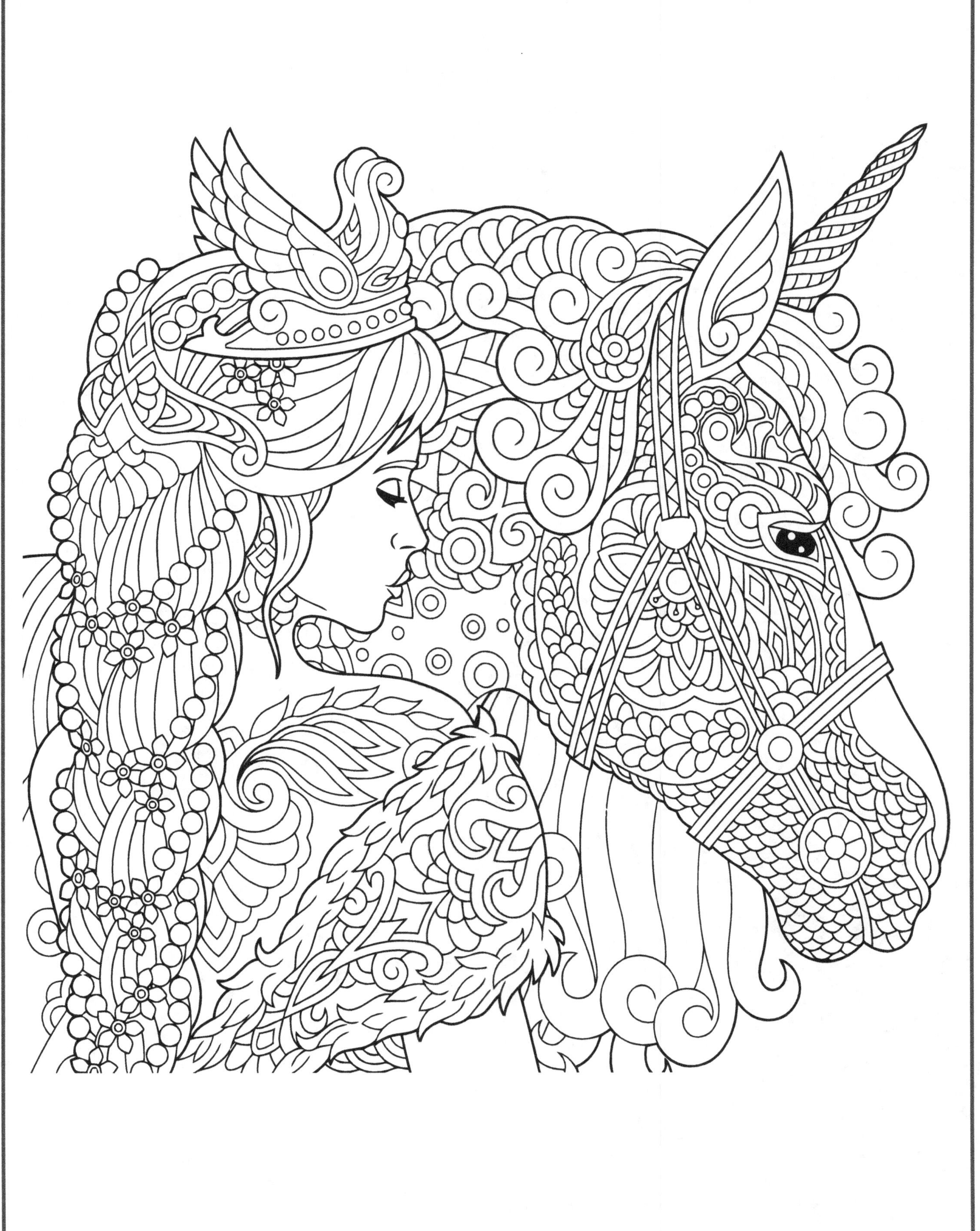

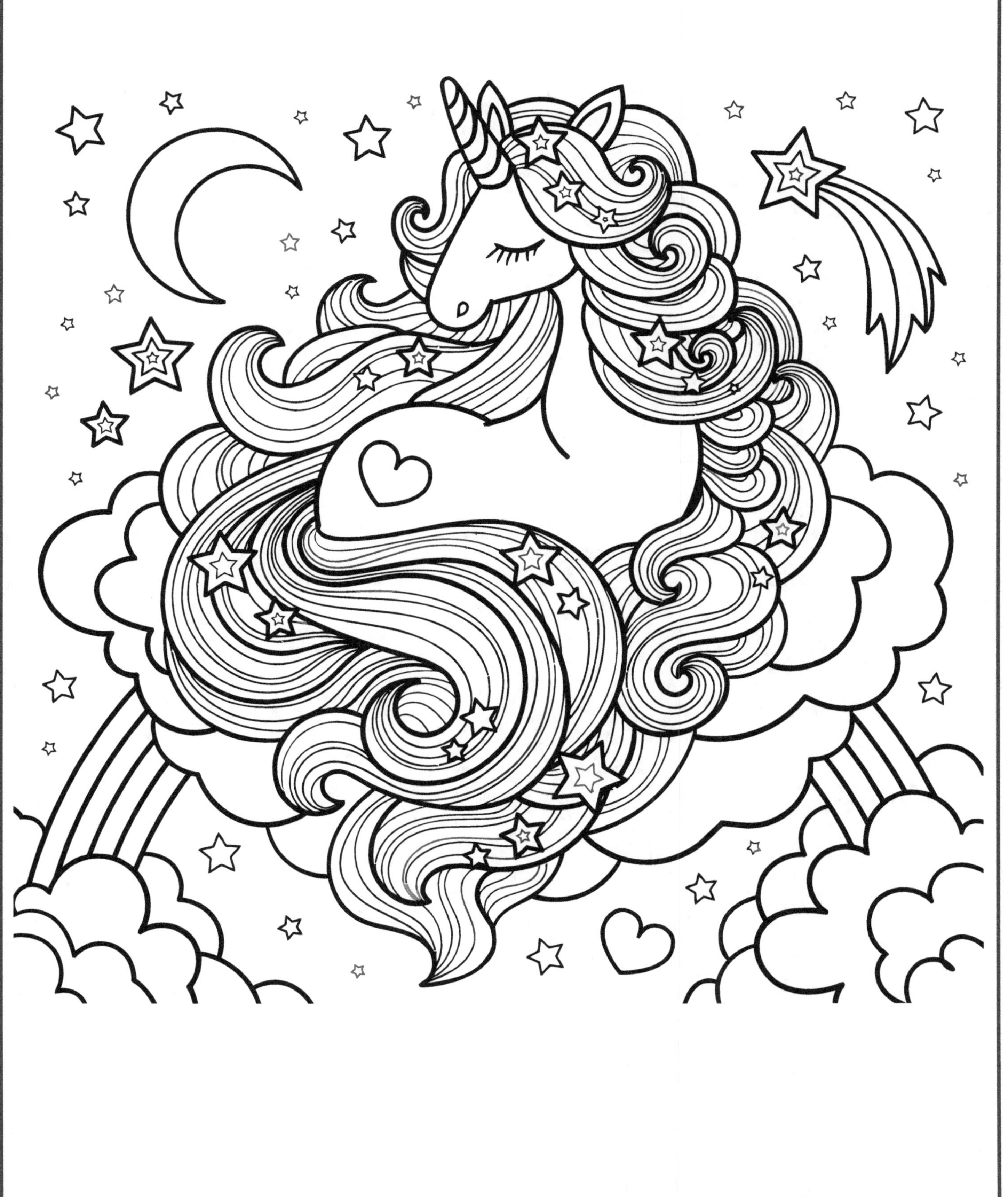

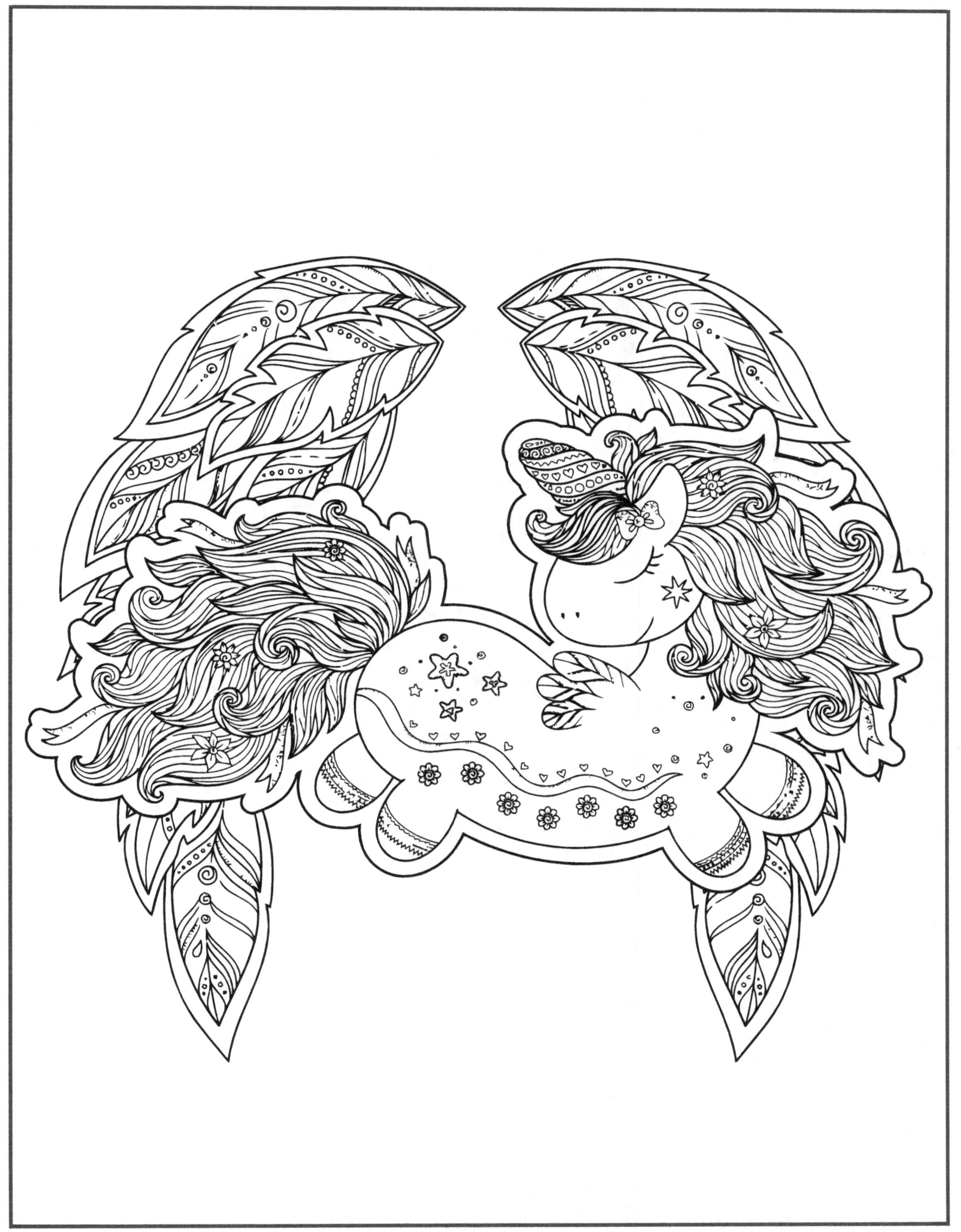

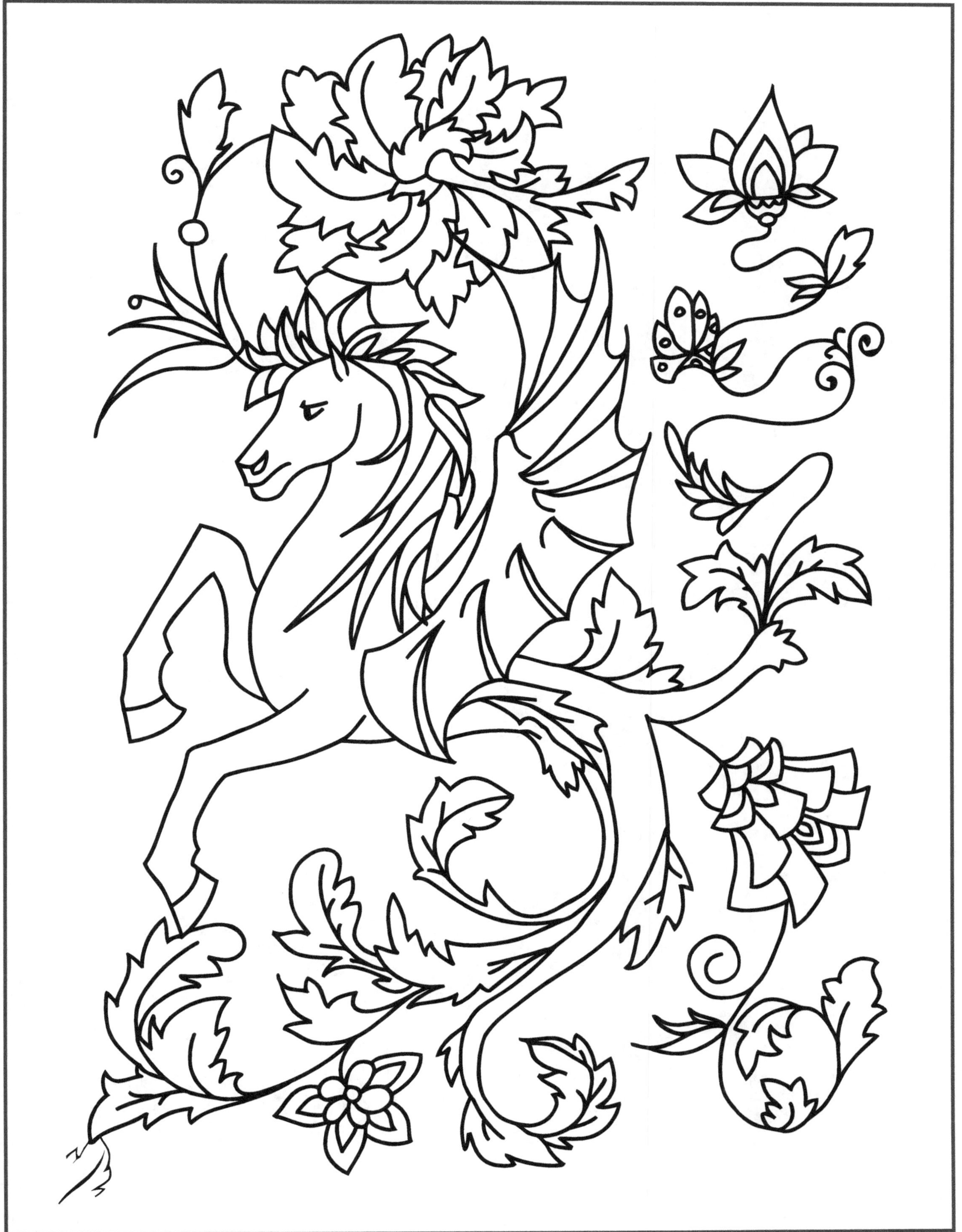

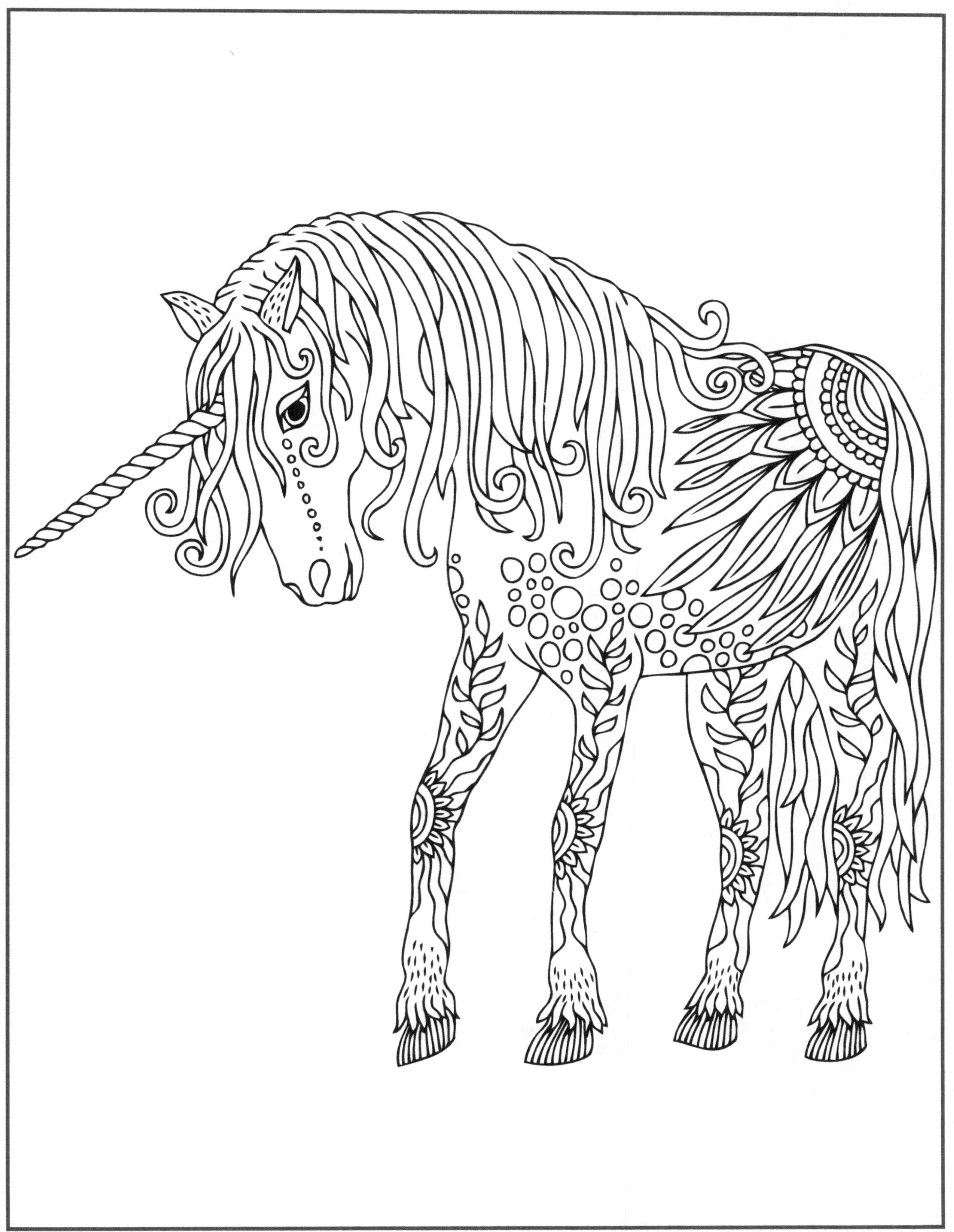

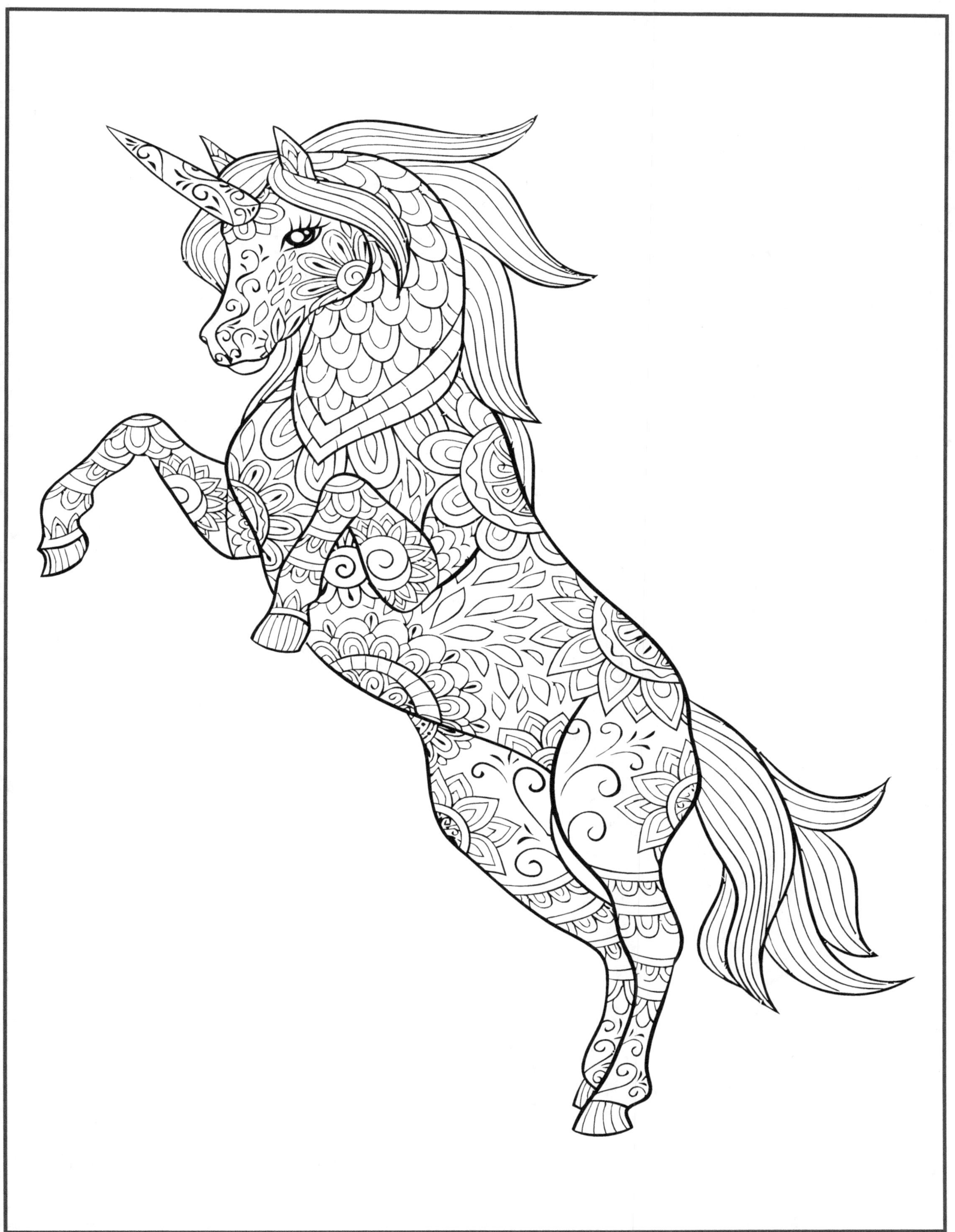

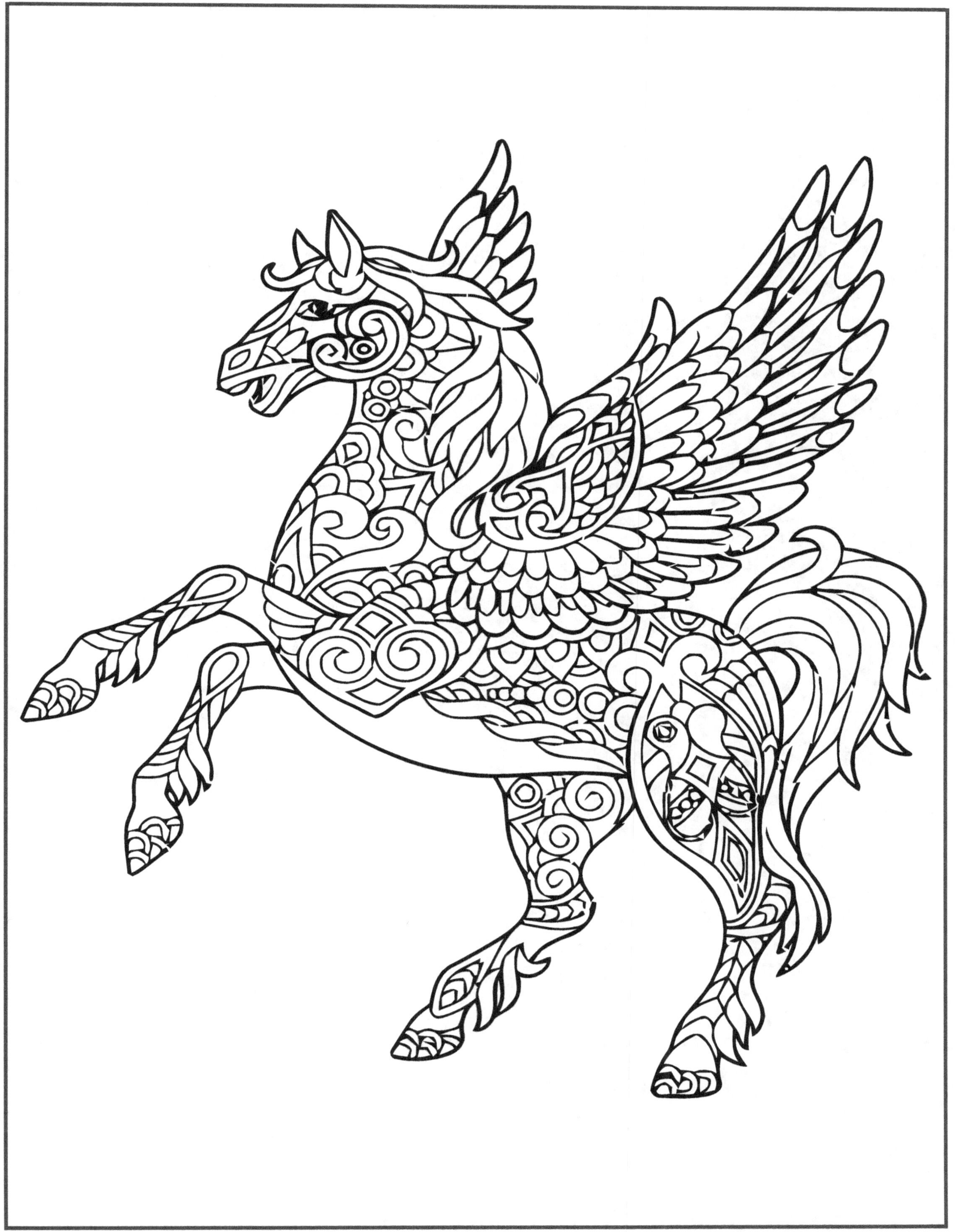

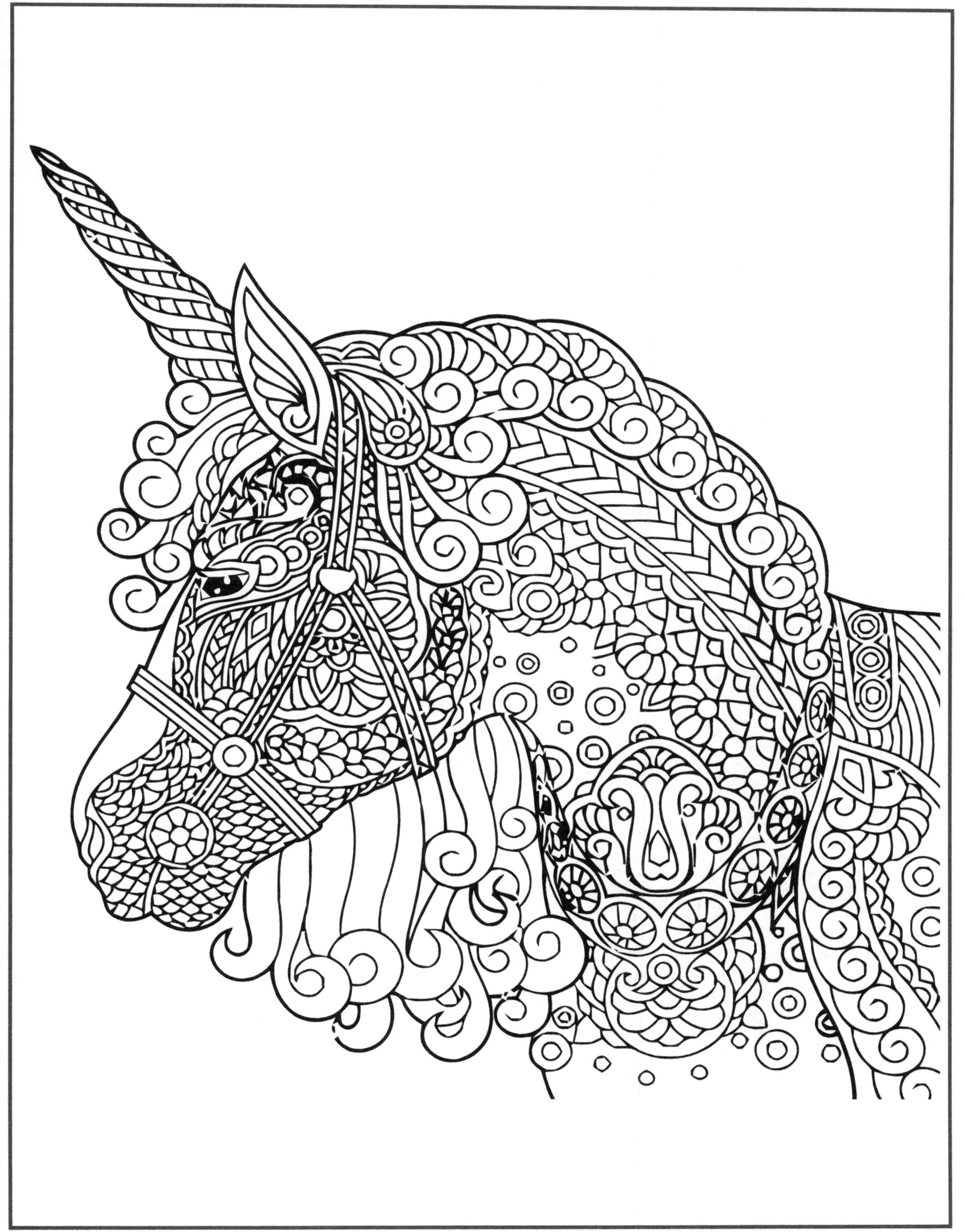

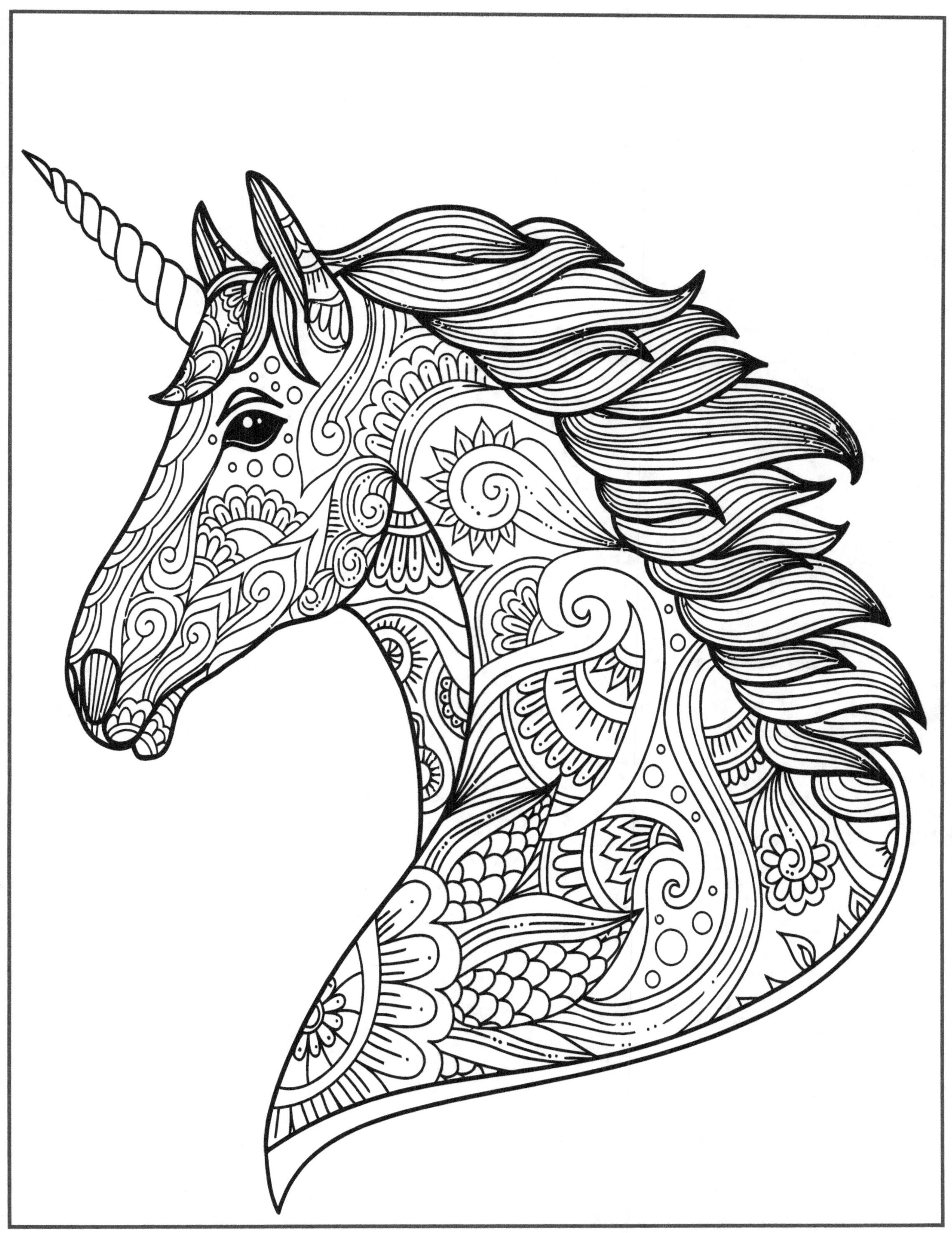

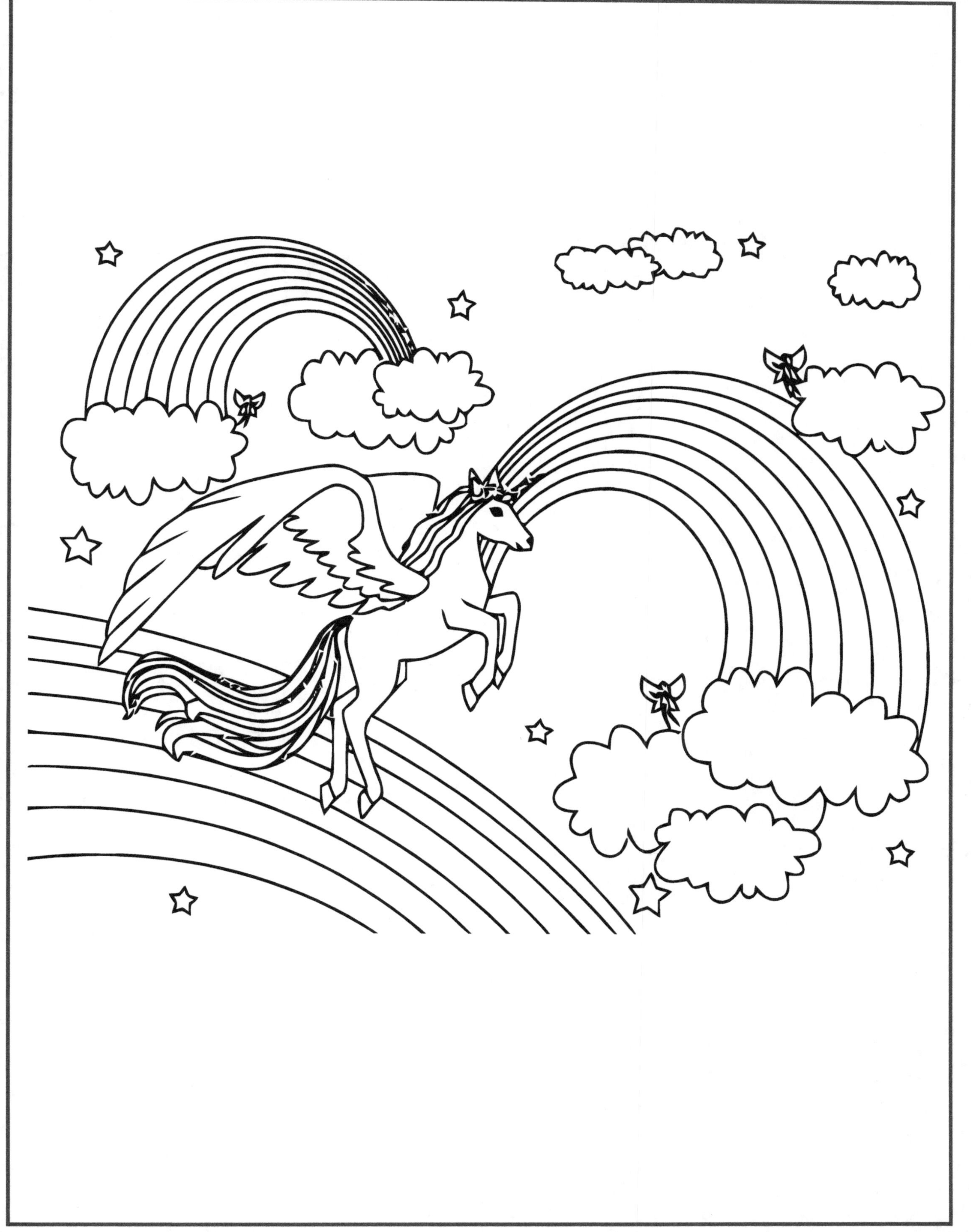

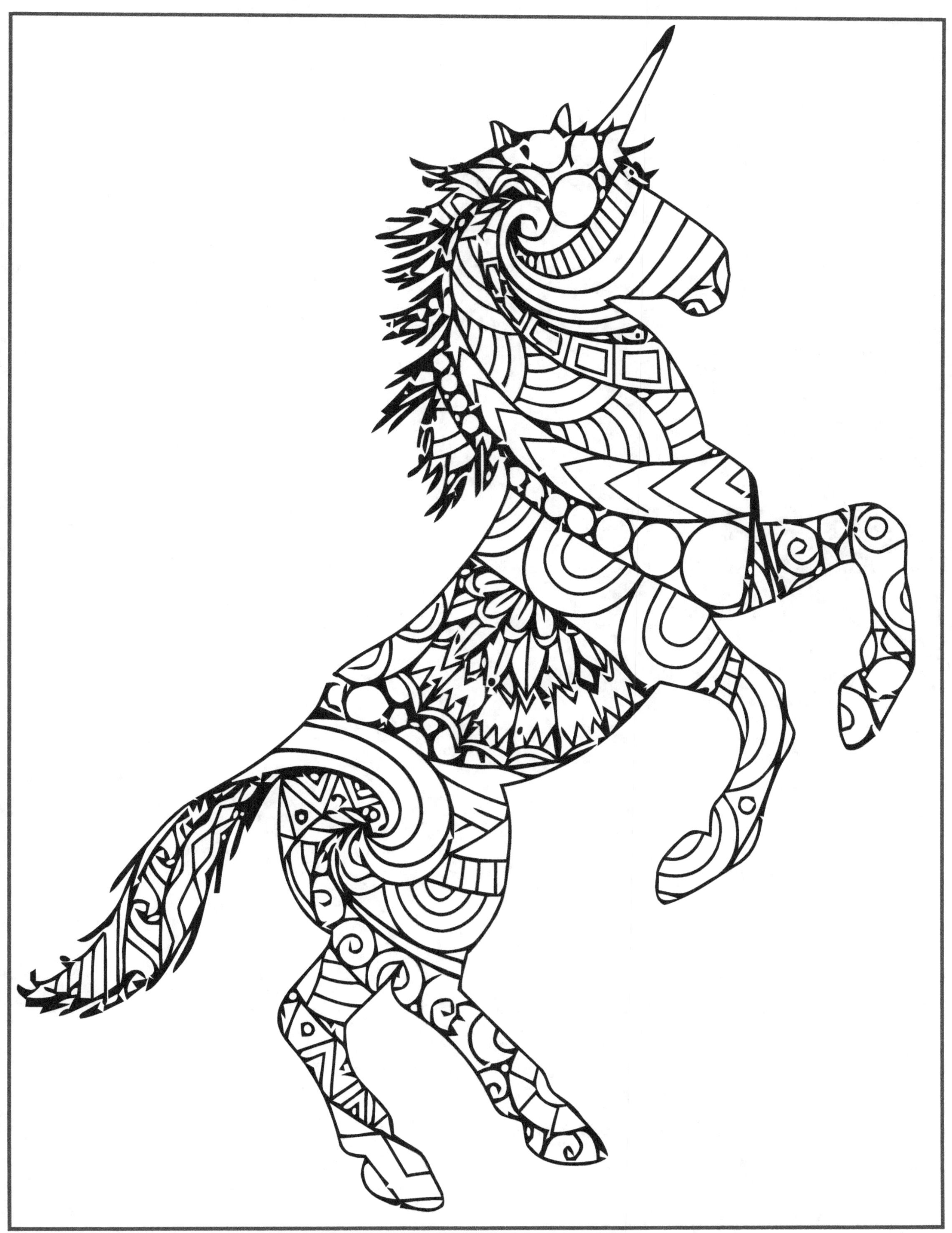

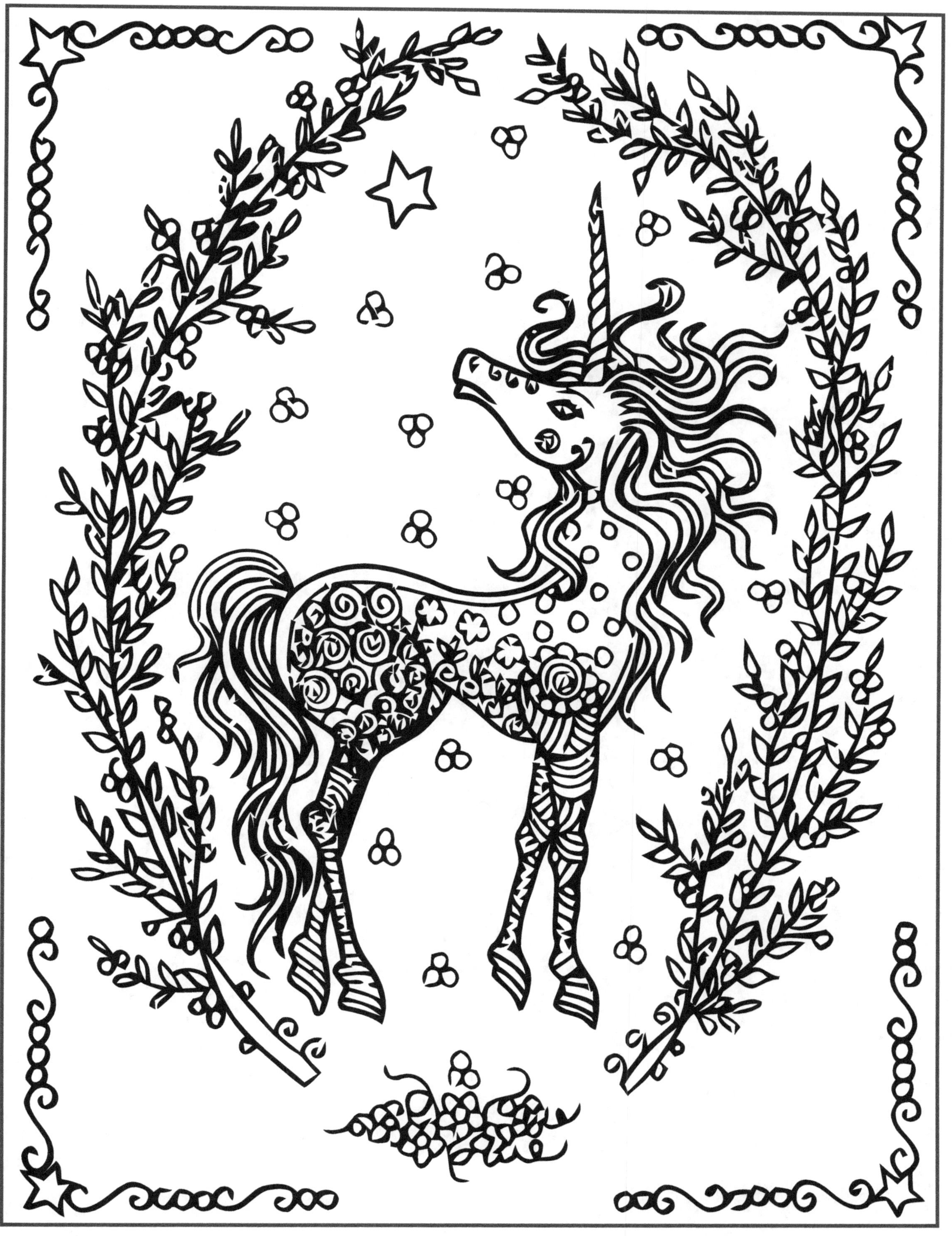

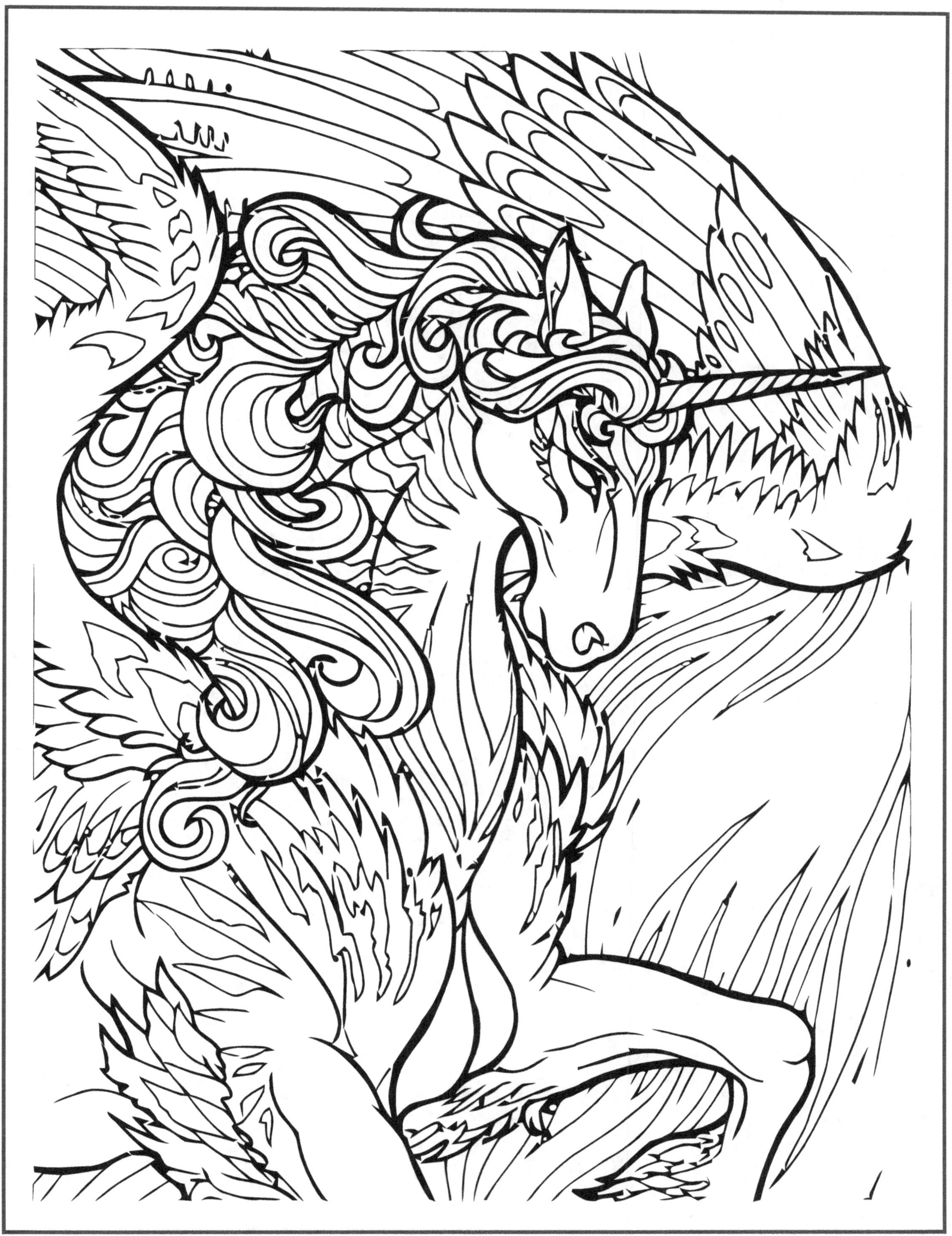

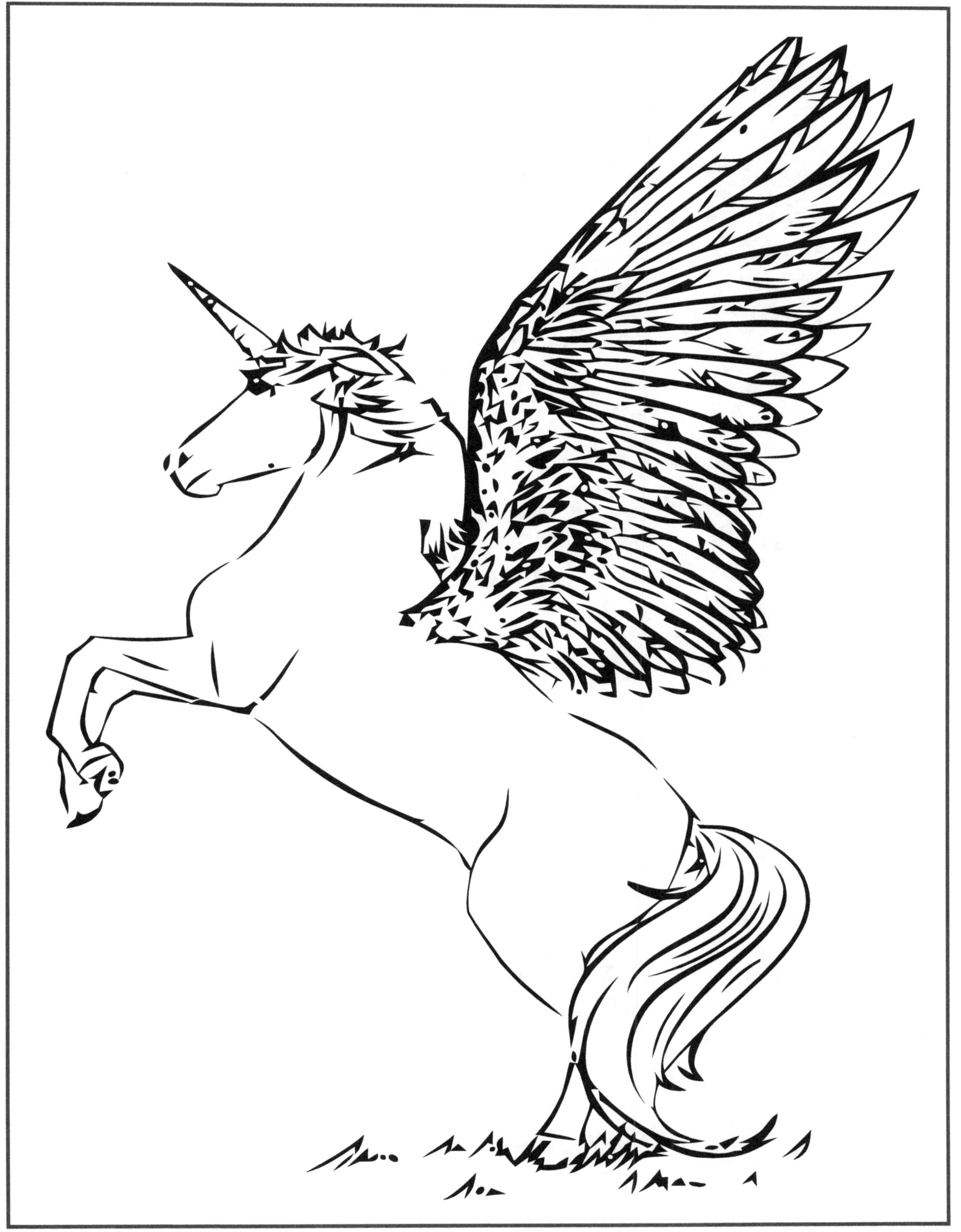

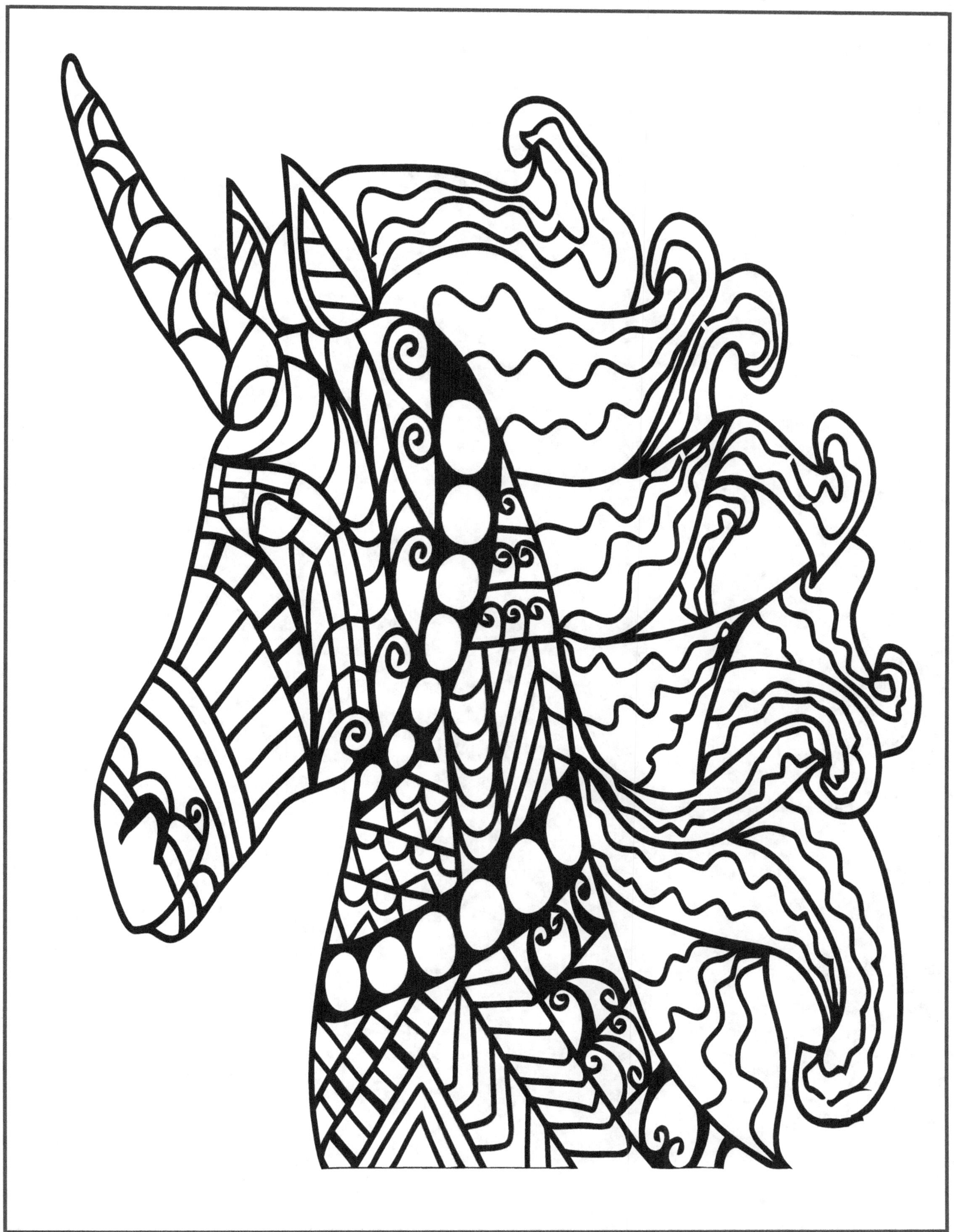

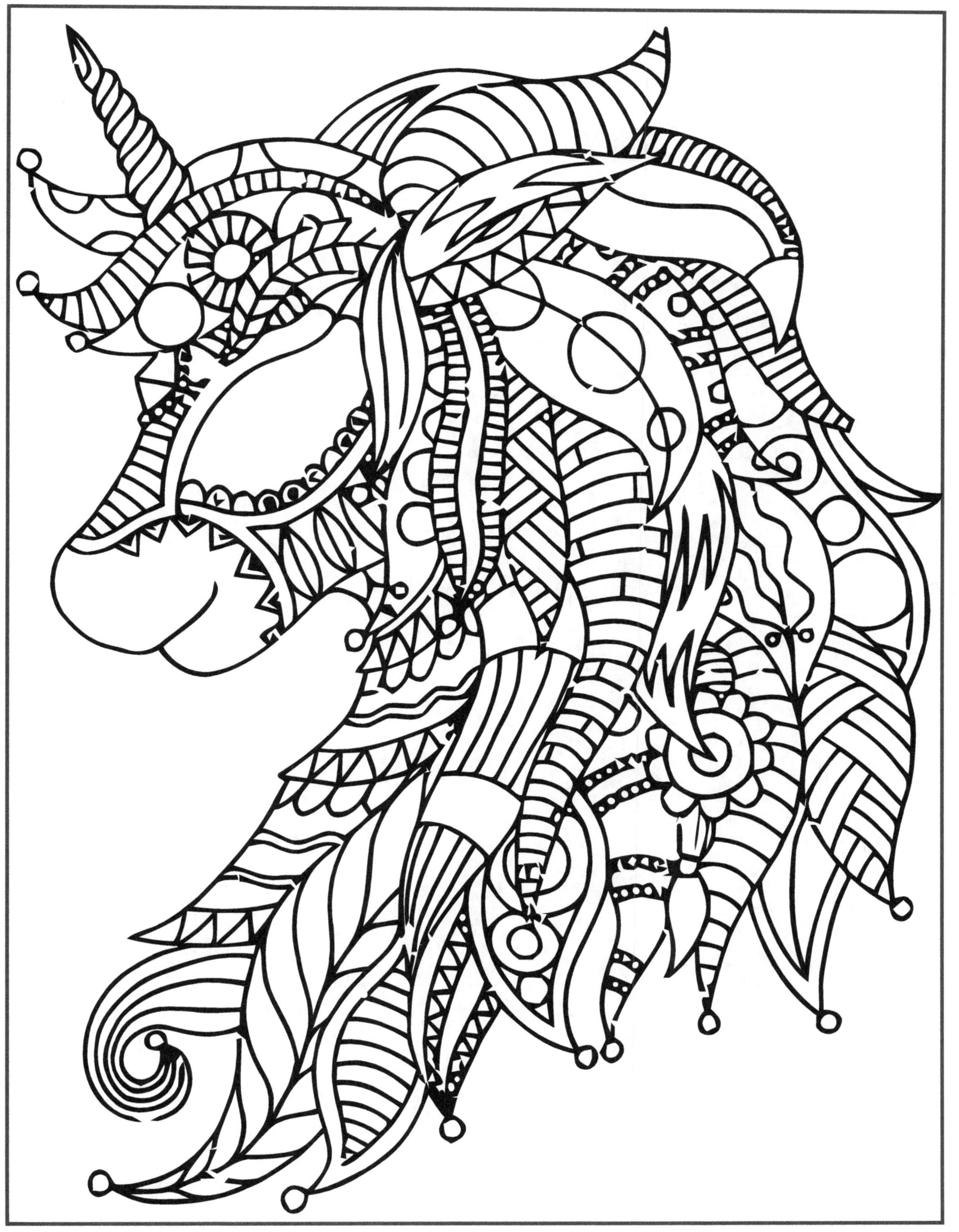

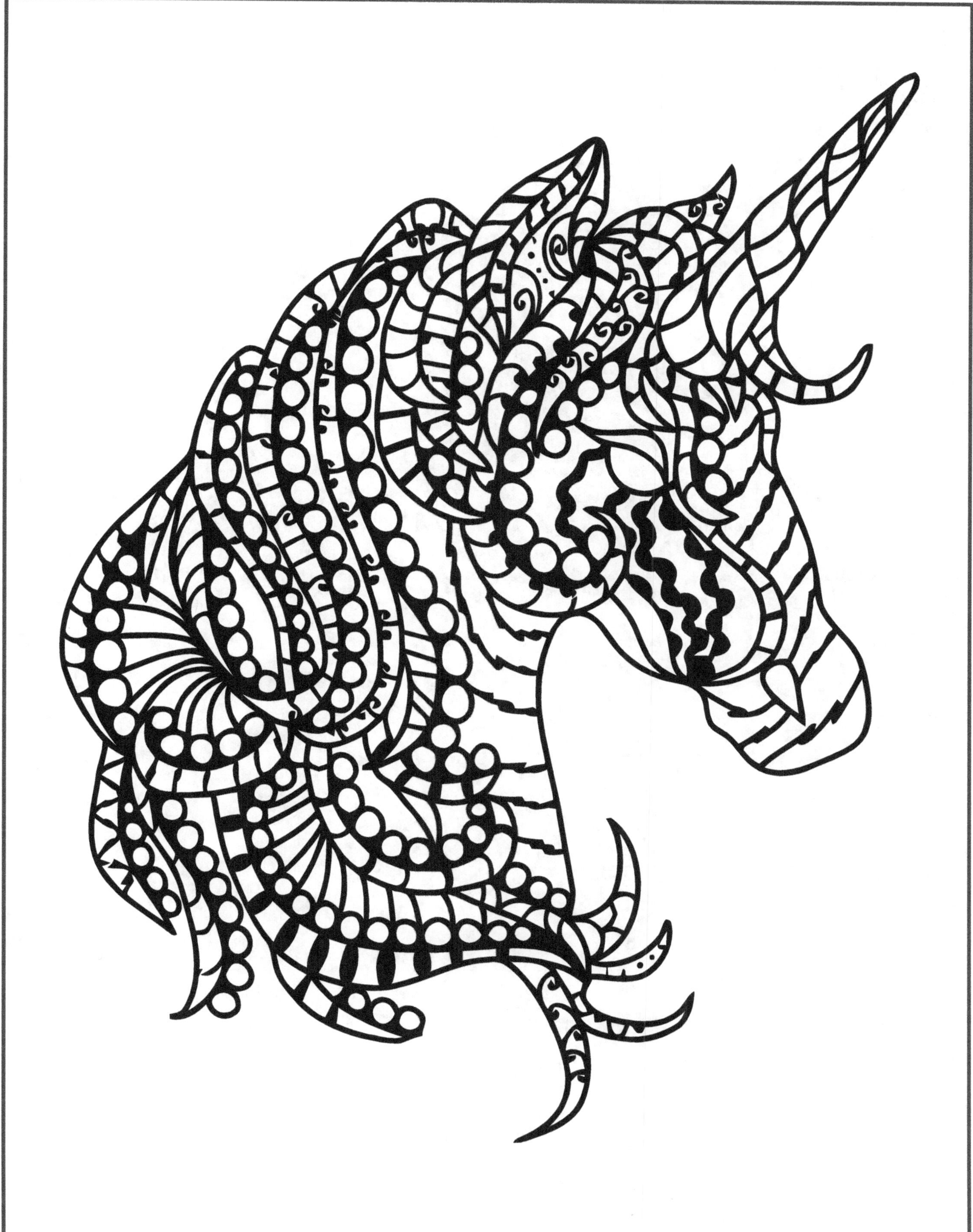

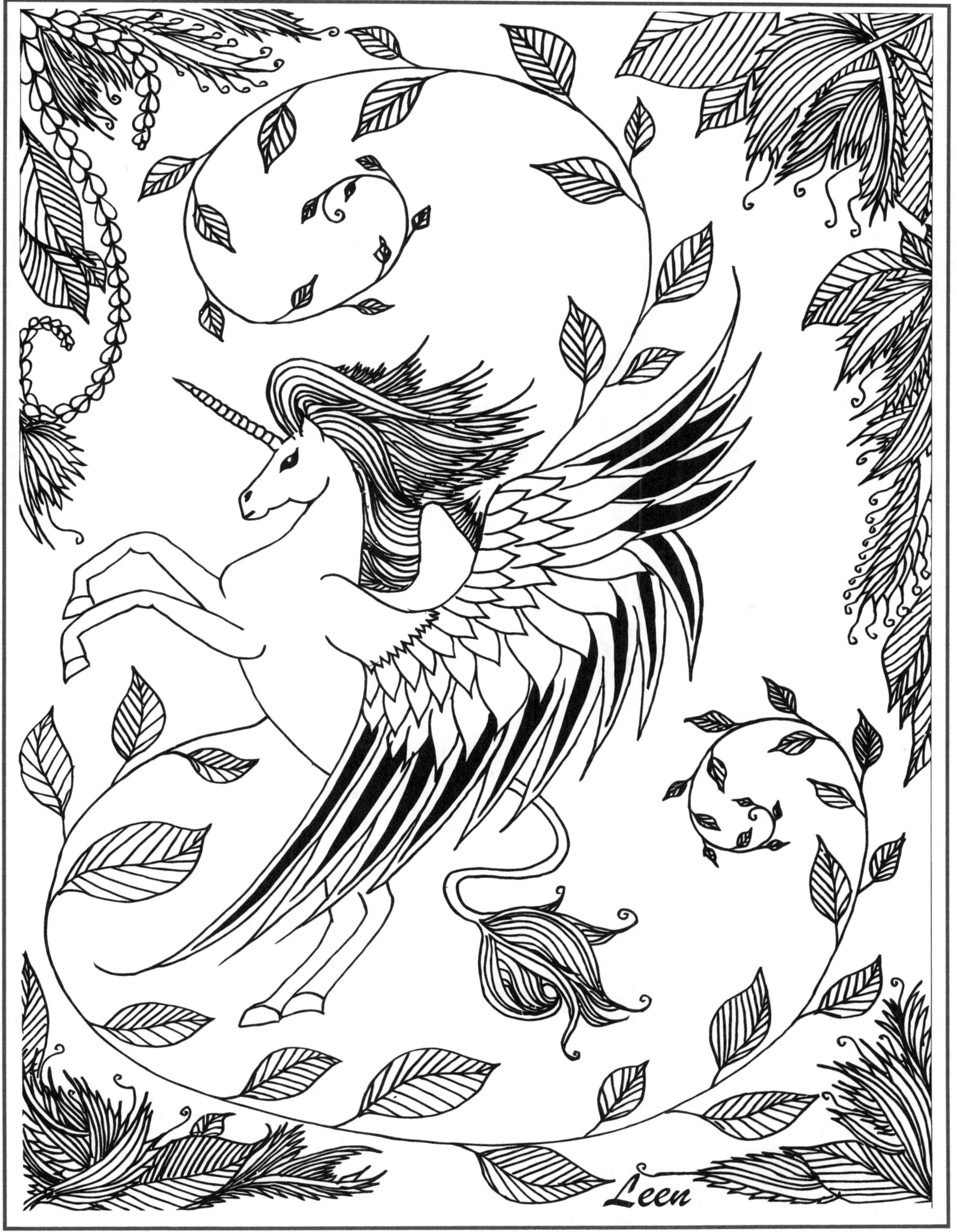
Leen

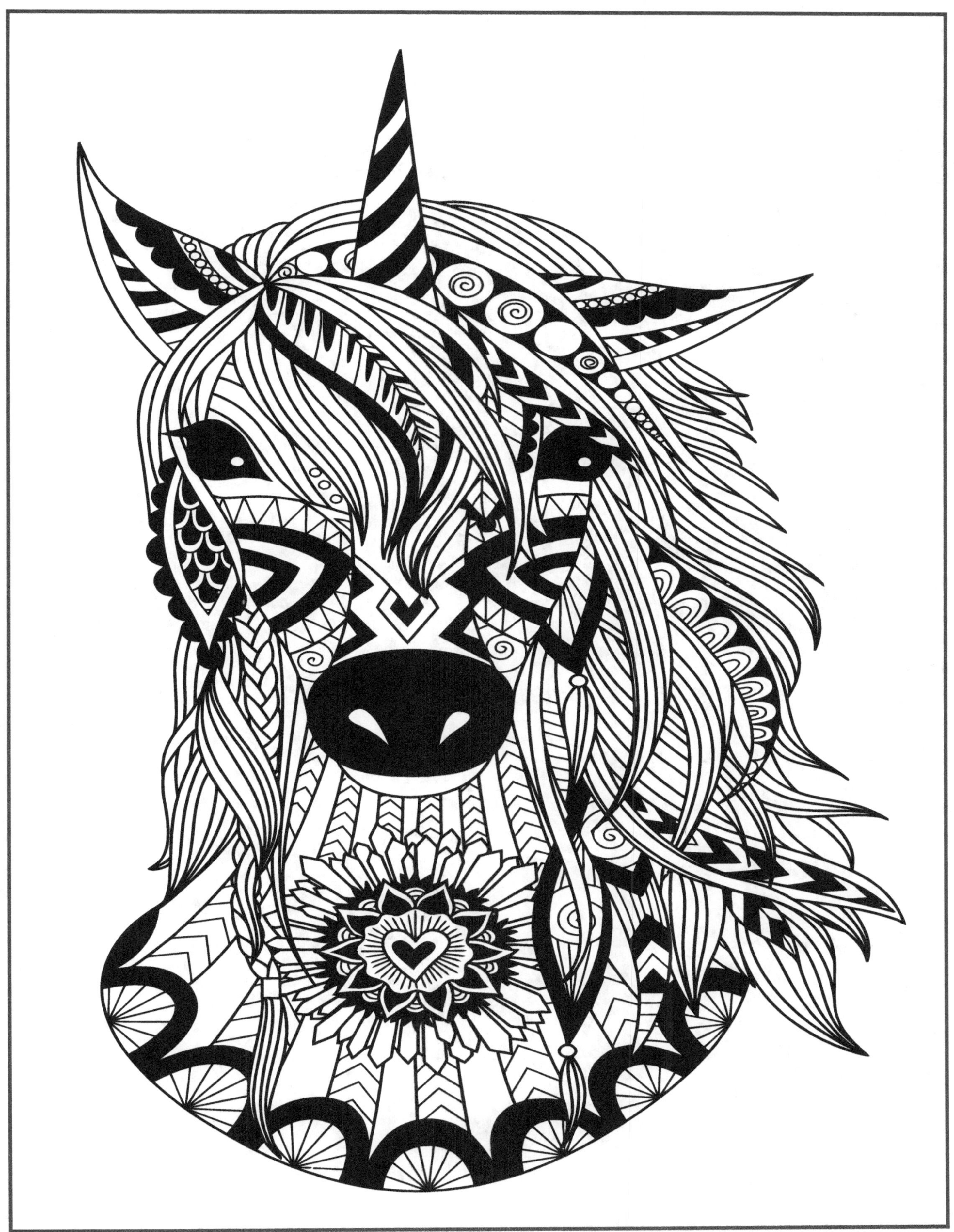